CANADIAN RAILROAD TRILOGY

Gordon Lightfoot

ART BY Ian Wallace

GROUNDWOOD BOOKS / HOUSE *of* ANANSI PRESS

TORONTO   BERKELEY

HERE WAS A TIME in this fair land when the railroad did not run,

When the wild majestic mountains stood alone against the sun.

Long before the white man and long before the wheel,

When the green dark forest was too silent to be real.

But time has no beginnings and history has no bounds,

As to this verdant country they came from all around.

They sailed upon her waterways and they walked the forest tall,

Built the mines, the mills and the factories for the good of us all.

And when the young man's fancy had turned him to the spring,
The railroad men grew restless for to hear the hammers ring.

Their minds were overflowing with the visions of their day,
With many a fortune won and lost and many a debt to pay.

For they looked in the future and what did they see,

They saw an iron road runnin' from the sea to the sea.

Bringin' the goods to a young growin' land,

All up from the seaports and into their hands.

"Look away," said they, "across this mighty land,

From the eastern shore to the western strand."

Bring in the workers and bring up the rails,
We gotta lay down the tracks and tear up the trails.

Open her heart, let the life blood flow,
Gotta get on our way 'cause we're movin' too slow.

Bring in the workers and bring up the rails,
We gotta lay down the tracks and tear up the trails.

Open her heart, let the life blood flow,
Gotta get on our way 'cause we're movin' too slow.
Get on our way 'cause we're movin' too slow.

Behind the blue Rockies the sun is declinin',

The stars they come stealin' at the close of the day.

Across the wide prairie our loved ones lie sleeping,

Beyond the dark oceans in a place far away.

We are the navvies who work upon the railway,

Swingin' our hammers in the bright blazin' sun.

Livin' on stew and drinkin' bad whiskey,

Bendin' our backs 'til the long day is done.

We are the navvies who work upon the railway,
Swingin' our hammers in the bright blazin' sun.

Layin' down track and buildin' the bridges,
Bendin' our backs 'til the railroad is done.

So over the mountains and over the plains,

Into the muskeg and into the rain.

Up the St. Lawrence all the way to Gaspé,

Swingin' our hammers and drawing our pay.

Drivin' 'em in and tyin' 'em down,
Away to the bunkhouse and into the town.

A dollar a day and a place for my head,
A drink to the livin', a toast to the dead.

Oh the song of the future has been sung,

All the battles have been won,

On the mountain tops we stand,
All the world at our command,

We have opened up the soil,
With our teardrops and our toil.

For there was a time in this fair land when the railroad did not run,

When the wild majestic mountains stood alone against the sun.

Long before the white man and long before the wheel,

When the green dark forest was too silent to be real.

When the green dark forest was too silent to be real.

And many are the dead men, too silent to be real.

CANADIAN RAILROAD TRILOGY

1. There was a time in this fair land when the rail-road did not run,
When the wild ma-jes-tic mount-ains stood a-lone a-gainst the sun.
Long be-fore the white man and long be-fore the wheel,
When the green dark fo-rest was too si-lent to be real.

But pay._____ 4. For they
looked in the fu-ture and what did they see,____ They saw an iron road
run-nin' from the sea to the sea.____ Bring-in' the goods____ to a
young grow-in' land,____ All up from the sea-ports and in-to their hands.__
"Look a-way,"____ said____ they,_____ "a-cross this migh-ty land,
From the eas-tern shore_____ to the wes-tern strand."__

2. But time has no beginnings and history has no bounds,
   As to this verdant country they came from all around.
   They sailed upon her waterways and they walked the forest tall,
   Built the mines, the mills and the factories for the good of us all.

3. And when the young man's fancy had turned him to the spring,
   The railroad men grew restless for to hear the hammers ring.
   Their minds were overflowing with the visions of their day,
   With many a fortune won and lost and many a debt to pay.

5. Bring in the workers and bring up the rails,
   We gotta lay down the tracks and tear up the trails.
   Open her heart, let the life blood flow,
   Gotta get on our way 'cause we're movin' too slow.
   Bring in the workers and bring up the rails,
   We gotta lay down the tracks and tear up the trails.
   Open her heart, let the life blood flow,
   Gotta get on our way 'cause we're movin' too slow.

Coda 1

ritard. - - - - - - - - - - - - -

E♭   Csus4   C

Get on our way___ 'cause we're mov-in' too slow.___

Moderately   F   F7   B♭   Csus4   F

6. Be - hind the blue Rock-ies the sun is___ de - clin-in', The stars they come

B♭   G   C   F   F7   B♭

steal-in' at the close of the day.___ A - cross the wide prai-rie our loved ones lie

Csus4   F   B♭   C   F

sleep-ing, Be - yond the dark o-ceans in a place far a - way.___

F7   B♭   Csus4

7. We are the nav-vies who work up - on the rail - way,

F   B♭   G   C   F

Swing-in' our ham-mers in the bright blaz-in' sun.___ Liv-in' on stew and

B♭   Csus4   **1.** F   B♭   Csus4   F

drink-in' bad whis-key, Bend-in' our backs 'til the long day is done.___

2. F   B♭   Csus4   C7

bend - in' our backs 'til the rail - road___ is

accel. - - - - - - - - - - - - - - - -

F   Cm7   F   Cm7   F

done.   9. So

8. We are the navvies who work upon the railway,
    Swingin' our hammers in the bright blazin' sun.
    Layin' down track and buildin' the bridges,
    Bendin' our backs 'til the railroad is done.

ov-er the moun - tains and ov-er the plains, ____ In-to the mus - keg and

in - to the rain. ____ Up the St. Law - rence all the way to Gas-pé, ____

Swing-in' our ham - mers and draw-ing our pay. ____ toast to the dead.

11. Oh the song of the fu-ture has been sung, All the bat-tles have been

won, On the moun-tain tops we stand, All the world at our com -

mand, We have o - pened up the soil, With our

tear - drops and our toil. ____ 12. For there

Coda 2

real. When the green dark fo - rest was too si - lent to be

real. And __ man-y are the dead men, _____ too

si - lent _____ to be real. _____

10. Drivin' 'em in and tyin' 'em down,
    Away to the bunkhouse and into the town.
    A dollar a day and a place for my head,
    A drink to the livin', a toast to the dead.

12. For there was a time in this fair land when the railroad did not run,
    When the wild majestic mountains stood alone against the sun.
    Long before the white man and long before the wheel,
    When the green dark forest was too silent to be real.

ILLUSTRATOR'S NOTES

I began this book where I always begin — with research. My starting point was Pierre Berton's acclaimed *The Last Spike*. Other sources followed.

An artist's pictures are only as good as the words the writer lays down. In this instance, Gordon Lightfoot's words opened up a wealth of possibilities for my imagination. I have loved the song and admired Lightfoot's music since I was a teenager growing up in the 1960s. He is a master storyteller, and the construction of the railroad is a thrilling saga.

For me, this is a song and a book about a dream — the dream of a prime minister and government, entrepreneurs and capitalists, engineers and workers, and the citizens of a young growing nation. I also recognize that for some, especially Canada's First People who were displaced by the railroad, and the navvies or workers (the vast majority of them Chinese immigrants) who suffered and died in the construction, the dream could be construed as a nightmare. The medium had to capture that dream and, as important, the magnificent but daunting landscape over which the railroad was built. It also had to evoke subtle elements like steam, mist, fog and wolves' hot breath, as well as rocky terrain and surfaces of steel.

Ultimately, I settled on handmade chalk pastels that I set down on gray pastel paper. I had never worked with the medium before and had limited knowledge of it. I hoped that it would capture the sweep of Lightfoot's song and Macdonald's dream. I also sought to convey my own vision, which I describe in the following notes.

A steam train heads into a tunnel as though entering the story about to be told. Tunnels through the Rockies were among the most difficult sections of the track to construct.

In this homage to French surrealist painter René Magritte, I have drawn a powerful piece of steel — the last spike.

Sir John A. Macdonald and his dream of a railroad running from sea to sea rise up in this image. The West Coast and Pacific appear on one side of the illustration and Percé Rock in the Gaspé Peninsula on the other.

The western terminus of the railroad was at Port Moody, British Columbia. This mountain scene includes a Salish totem pole to honor the people who have lived in this region for thousands of years.

To capture a forest that was "too silent to be real," I set this illustration on a cold summer night, imagining the Woodlands people inside their wigwams, settled around fires for warmth.

This drawing spans a thousand years in the history of people coming to Canada, including an eleventh-century Viking ship on its way to L'Anse aux Meadows, Newfoundland, a nineteenth-century French sailing ship, a twentieth-century British vessel of the Cunard Line and a twenty-first-century jet plane.

The line "sailed upon her waterways" made me think of the physical obstacles that early explorers of the New World had to overcome. Franciscan priests are credited with being the first Europeans to see Niagara Falls in the seventeenth century.

Men in top hats are reminiscent of the pollution-causing smokestacks and chimneys of trains and industry. Mostly I show anonymous men, unsung engineers and other railroad professionals, but I have also included, from left to right, front row: #3 George Stephen, president of the CPR; #5 Andrew Onderdonk, contractor overseeing the section of track between Port Moody and Savona's Ferry, British Columbia; #6 William Cornelius Van Horne, general manager of the CPR (and later vice president and president); and #10 Major A.B. Rogers, the engineer who discovered Rogers Pass.

A contemporary, young First Nations girl races an early train across the fertile prairie, bringing together the present and the past.

Men unload goods from a train at an East Coast station. The railroad was designed to ensure East-West trade across the country.

I wondered what it was like for First Nations children to watch an endless stream of covered wagons roll through their valleys. Virga, or precipitation that evaporates before it reaches the ground, can be seen falling from the cloud in this typical western sky.

Before they could build the track, workers had to clear a path through the forest. Then they laid down heavy wooden ties that were hammered into place with iron spikes. I have drawn a man wearing a beaded glove in the left-hand corner in memory of the First Nations people who worked on the railway.

In this drawing, north of Lake Superior, I wanted to acknowledge the thousands of navvies who worked on the railroad and were recognized as being extremely hard and reliable workers.

This winter scene of wolves in the Rockies shows some of the magnificent landscape through which the railway was built. The ambitious construction inevitably disrupted wildlife and the natural world.

The majority of the navvies who dug the tunnels and built the mountain passes in the Rockies were from China. These men, more than seven thousand strong, paid an enormous and often fatal price for their jobs. Incredibly, the new nation rewarded these workers, without whom the railroad could not have been built, with racism — a head tax on Chinese immigration. The "dream" image pays homage to these men and their families. A man sleeps atop a dragon's head dreaming of his wife and several symbols from his past, among them the Temple of Heaven, the mountains around the Li River, Guilin, and the Chinese character for home.

Here the railway workers appear larger than life, like heroes, set against an iconic grain elevator and a vast prairie sky.

Navvies spend an evening relaxing, drinking and singing as snow falls outside. Gordon Lightfoot circa the 1970s is the navvy singing on the far right of the bunkhouse.

An imaginary Gold Mountain rises out of the fog and cloud behind one of the many trestle bridges. The huge wooden trestles, remarkable feats of engineering, were temporary structures, which were later replaced with steel and concrete.

The section of track that crosses the muskeg at Jackfish Bay, northern Ontario, was one of the most difficult and expensive to construct. Rock fill in muskeg sinks until it becomes stable. This section alone reportedly cost $700,000, including a tunnel not shown in the illustration. The minimal palette in this scene emphasizes the miserable weather.

Intended to be a sharp contrast to the previous scene, this drawing illustrates another heroic figure set against the typical clouds and brilliant light of the East Coast.

During my research, I read that where railway men went, the women of the night followed. So I have alluded to this reality. I was also intrigued to learn that the workers were willing to walk up to 10 miles (16 km) to buy a beer.

It was essential that I acknowledge the enormous change that came to the lives of Canada's First People, their contribution to the railroad's construction, and the price they paid for the iron road that crossed their land. I have represented this symbolically. A lone buffalo confronts a train called Progress, a train that brought with it the arrival of a prime minister's national dream and the decimation of a people and a culture. A map of Canada, the formation of a nation, appears in the cloud of smoke coming from the train.

On a humorous note, this image illustrates the moment the navvies stood "On the mountain tops ... All the world at our command." I recalled that when the CN Tower was completed in Toronto, in 1975, several workers relieved themselves from that great height. Apparently it is often the custom when the construction of a skyscraper is finished.

A Salish girl stands against a totem pole contemplating the change coming to her people, as the sun sets on the world she knows and is about to rise on an uncertain future.

This image showing geese flying over the St. Lawrence River depicts a time when Canada was covered by pristine forests, lakes and rivers.

Many men perished in the building of the railroad. One man died for every mile of the line between Vancouver and Calgary, mostly due to dynamite explosions in the Rocky Mountains. I have laid five of those men to rest in the shelter of Rogers Pass, British Columbia. The pinkish tone beneath the glacier was intended to reflect the sky, but also to suggest the blood spilled during the construction. In the summertime, a species of algae commonly known as watermelon snow creates this same pink tone on glaciers.

The final drawing shows a train just beginning to emerge from a tunnel — the end of the story. The beauty and range of the chalk pastels enabled me to imagine billowing steam contrasted against the dark background of steel and rock.

And a final note regarding the medium — chalk pastels are highly tactile. The blending and shading in this book were accomplished with the baby and middle fingers of my left hand.

— Ian Wallace

THE CANADIAN PACIFIC RAILWAY – A BRIEF HISTORY

In 1871 Canada's first prime minister, Sir John A. Macdonald, promised British Columbia that if it joined Confederation, he would build a railway out to the Pacific Coast. Railway lines already existed in the eastern part of the country, but there was nothing that linked the East and West. The government was also concerned that trade would take place between North and South. A railroad would ensure that Canadians settled the West.

The government eventually hired Andrew Onderdonk, an American contractor, to begin work on the railroad in British Columbia. The plan was to lay the track in both directions at once. Surveyors began to search for a route through a wilderness that included the hard rock of the Canadian Shield, swampy muskeg and rugged mountain ranges.

In 1881 the Canadian Pacific Railway (CPR) was established as a private company, with generous government support, and George Stephen became president. A year later he hired American William Van Horne to manage the construction of the railroad. Van Horne was determined to build faster than ever before. Under his supervision thousands upon thousands of workers cleared trees, leveled land, built bridges and blasted through rock with dynamite. Then they laid the track.

Many of the workers, or navvies, came from Europe, Russia and China. They ate and slept in bunkhouses, tents or even railway cars (referred to as "End of Track"). The navvies were paid between $1 and $2.50 a day. Chinese navvies, who worked mainly on the stretch of railway in British Columbia, were paid the lowest wages even though they usually performed the most dangerous and difficult tasks. Hundreds lost their lives in accidents or because they fell ill, and many were too poor to ever return to their home countries.

The last spike was hammered in place on November 7, 1885, at Craigellachie, British Columbia, joining the rails from east to west. The first steam train to carry passengers across the country traveled from Montreal to Port Moody, British Columbia, in 1886.

The benefits of the railroad were many. It provided employment. It made land travel far easier and made cross-country communication possible, since telegraph lines were built along the track. The government and the CPR encouraged thousands of immigrants and others to settle the West, offering them land either for free or for a good price. Trains were also used to transport manufactured goods west and cattle, wheat, wood and coal east. Stations were built all along the track, and new towns and eventually cities grew up around them. Tourism flourished. The Canadian Pacific Railway played an essential role in building and shaping a young nation.

But for all it brought the new Canada, the railroad had a devastating effect on the Métis and First Nations people. The land that the government granted to the CPR and to settlers was their land — the land where they had long lived and hunted. Many First Nations were already struggling due to the overhunting of buffalo by whites. Now they were forced to move onto reserves. This loss of their traditional way of life and culture has never been repaired.

FURTHER READING

Ancient Thunder by Leo Yerxa. Groundwood Books, 2006.

Canada Moves West by Pierre Berton, foreword by Arthur Slade. Fifth House, 2005.

Ghost Train by Paul Yee, illustrated by Harvey Chan. Groundwood Books, 1996, 2009.

The Kids Book of Canada's Railway and How the CPR Was Built by Deborah Hodge, illustrated by John Mantha. Kids Can Press, 2000.

A Ribbon of Shining Steel: The Railway Diary of Kate Cameron by Julie Lawson. Scholastic Canada, 2002.

Tales from Gold Mountain: Stories of the Chinese in the New World by Paul Yee, paintings by Simon Ng. Groundwood Books, 1989.

The artist and publisher would like to thank Jo-Anne Colby of the Canadian Pacific Archives for her helpful comments.

For Deb, as always and ever, but also with appreciation to my Boston friends, whose support and enthusiasm throughout this project kept me drawing with inspiration and passion. I love you all. Mary Lee and Ed, Lorna and Jeannie, Jaylyn and Dale, Marshall and Sandy, and Justin and Dora. — IW

Canadian Railroad Trilogy • Words and Music by Gordon Lightfoot
© 1967 (Renewed) Moose Music Ltd. Used by Permission of
Alfred Music Publishing Co, Inc.
All rights reserved.
Illustrations copyright © 2010 by Ian Wallace
Published in Canada and the USA in 2010 by Groundwood Books

We acknowledge for their financial support of our publishing program the Canada Council for the Arts, the Government of Canada through the Canada Book Fund (CBF) and the Ontario Arts Council.

Groundwood Books / House of Anansi Press
110 Spadina Avenue, Suite 801, Toronto, Ontario M5V 2K4
or c/o Publishers Group West
1700 Fourth Street, Berkeley, CA 94710

Library and Archives Canada Cataloguing in Publication

Lightfoot, Gordon
Canadian railroad trilogy / written by Gordon Lightfoot ; illustrated by Ian Wallace.
ISBN 978-0-88899-953-5
1. Canadian Pacific Railway Company—History—Juvenile literature.
2. Railroads—Canada—History—Juvenile literature. I. Wallace, Ian II. Title.
PS8573.I42C36 2010   jC811'.54   C2010-902450-8

Photography by Trent Photographics
Design by Michael Solomon
Printed and bound in China by Everbest Printing Co. Ltd.

Canada Council   Conseil des Arts
for the Arts   du Canada

ONTARIO ARTS COUNCIL
CONSEIL DES ARTS DE L'ONTARIO